Medea

EURIPIDES

Published in 1910

TABLE OF CONTENTS

DRAMATIS PERSONAE

NURSE OF MEDEA.
ATTENDANT ON HER CHILDREN.
MEDEA.
CHORUS OF CORINTHIAN WOMEN.
CREON.
JASON.
ÆGEUS.
MESSENGER.
THE TWO SONS OF JASON AND MEDEA.

MEDEA

SCENE.
Before the Palace of Creon at Corinth.

NURSE. Ah! would to Heaven the good ship Argo ne'er had sped its course to the Colchian land through the misty blue Symplegades, nor ever in the glens of Pelion the pine been felled to furnish with oars the chieftain's hands, who went to fetch the golden fleece for Pelias; for then would my own mistress Medea never have sailed to the turrets of Iolcos, her soul with love for Jason smitten, nor would she have beguiled the daughters of Pelias to slay their father and come to live here in the land of Corinth with her husband and children, where her exile found favour with the citizens to whose land she had come, and in all things of her own accord was she at one with Jason, the greatest safeguard this when wife and husband do agree; but now their love is all turned to hate, and tenderest ties are weak. For Jason hath betrayed his own children and my mistress dear for the love of a royal bride, for he hath wedded the daughter of Creon, lord of this land. While Medea his hapless wife, thus scorned, appeals to the oaths he swore, recalls the strong pledge his right hand gave, and bids heaven be witness what requital she is finding from Jason. And here she lies fasting, yielding her body to her grief, wasting away in tears ever since she learnt that she was wronged by her husband, never lifting her eye nor raising her face from off the ground; and she lends as deaf an ear to her friend's warning as if she were a rock or ocean billow, save when she turns her snow-white neck aside and softly to herself bemoans her father dear, her country and her home, which she gave up to come hither with the man who now holds her in dishonour. She, poor lady, hath by sad experience learnt how good a thing it is never to quit one's native land. And she hates her children now and feels no joy at seeing them; I am afeard she may contrive some untoward scheme; for her mood is dangerous nor will she brook her cruel treatment; full well I know her, and I much do dread that she will plunge the keen sword through their heart, stealing without a word into the chamber where their marriage couch is spread, or else that she will slay the prince and bridegroom too, and so find some calamity still more grievous than the present; for dreadful is her wrath; verily the man that doth incur her hate will have no easy task to raise o'er her a song of triumph. Lo! where her sons come hither from their childish sports; little they reck of their mother's woes, for the soul of the young is no friend to sorrow.

ATTENDANT. Why dost thou, so long my lady's own handmaid, stand here at the gate alone, loudly lamenting to thyself the piteous tale? how comes it that Medea will have thee leave her to herself?

NURSE. Old man, attendant on the sons of Jason, our masters' fortunes when they go awry make good slaves grieve and touch their hearts. Oh! I have come to such a pitch of grief that there stole a yearning wish upon me to come forth hither and proclaim to heaven and earth my mistress's hard fate.

ATTENDANT. What! has not the poor lady ceased yet from her lamentation?

NURSE. Would I were as thou art! the mischief is but now beginning; it has not reached its climax yet.

ATTENDANT. O foolish one, if I may call my mistress such a name; how little she recks of evils yet more recent!

NURSE. What mean'st, old man? grudge not to tell me.

ATTENDANT. 'Tis naught; I do repent me even of the words I have spoken.

NURSE. Nay, by thy beard I conjure thee, hide it not from thy fellow-slave; I will be silent, if need be, on that text.

ATTENDANT. I heard one say, pretending not to listen as I approached the place where our greybeards sit playing draughts [1] near Pirene's sacred spring, that Creon, the ruler of this land, is bent on driving these children and their mother from the boundaries of Corinth; but I know not whether the news is to be relied upon, and would fain it were not.

NURSE. What! will Jason brook such treatment of his sons, even though he be at variance with their mother?

ATTENDANT. Old ties give way to new; he bears no longer any love to this family.

NURSE. Undone, it seems, are we, if to old woes fresh ones we add, ere we have drained the former to the dregs.

ATTENDANT. Hold thou thy peace, say not a word of this; 'tis no time for our mistress to learn hereof.

NURSE. O children, do ye hear how your father feels towards you?

Perdition catch him, but no! he is my master still; yet is he proved a very traitor to his nearest and dearest.

ATTENDANT. And who 'mongst men is not? Art learning only now, that every single man cares for himself more than for his neighbour, some from honest motives, others for mere gain's sake? seeing that to indulge his passion their father has ceased to love these children.

NURSE. Go, children, within the house; all will be well. Do thou keep them as far away as may be, and bring them not near their mother in her evil hour. For ere this have I seen her eyeing them savagely, as though she were minded to do them some hurt, and well I know she will not cease from her fury till she have pounced on some victim. At least may she turn her hand against her foes, and not against her friends.

MEDEA. (within). Ah, me! a wretched suffering woman I! O would that I could die!

NURSE. 'Tis as I said, my dear children; wild fancies stir your mother's heart, wild fury goads her on. Into the house without delay, come not near her eye, approach her not, beware her savage mood, the fell tempest of her reckless heart. In, in with what speed ye may. For 'tis plain she will soon redouble her fury; that cry is but the herald of the gathering storm-cloud whose lightning soon will flash; what will her proud restless soul, in the anguish of despair, be guilty of?

[Exit Attendant with the children.

MEDEA. (within). Ah, me! the agony I have suffered, deep enough to call for these laments! Curse you and your father too, ye children damned, sons of a doomed mother! Ruin seize the whole family!

NURSE. Ah me! ah me! the pity of it! Why, pray, do thy children share their father's crime? Why hatest thou them? Woe is you, poor children, how do I grieve for you lest ye suffer some outrage! Strange are the tempers of princes, and maybe because they seldom have to obey, and mostly lord it over others, change they their moods with difficulty. 'Tis better then to have been trained to live on equal terms. Be it mine to reach old age, not in proud pomp, but in security! Moderation wins the day first as a better word for men to use, and likewise it is far the best course for them to pursue; but greatness that doth o'erreach itself, brings no blessing to mortal men; but pays a penalty of greater ruin whenever fortune is wroth with a family.

CHORUS. I heard the voice, uplifted loud, of our poor Colchian lady, nor yet is she quiet; speak, aged dame, for as I stood by the house with double gates I heard a voice of weeping from within, and I do grieve, lady, for the sorrows of this house, for it hath won my love.

NURSE. 'Tis a house no more; all that is passed away long since; a royal bride keeps Jason at her side, while our mistress pines away in her bower, finding no comfort for her soul in aught her friends can say.

MEDEA. (within). Oh, oh! Would that Heaven's levin bolt would cleave this head in twain! What gain is life to me? Woe, woe is me! O, to die and win release, quitting this loathed existence!

CHORUS. Didst hear, O Zeus, thou earth, and thou, O light, the piteous note of woe the hapless wife is uttering? How shall a yearning for that insatiate[2]resting-place ever hasten for thee, poor reckless one, the end that death alone can bring? Never pray for that. And if thy lord prefers a fresh love, be not angered with him for that; Zeus will judge 'twixt thee and him herein. Then mourn not for thy husband's loss too much, nor waste thyself away.

MEDEA. (within). Great Themis, and husband[3] of Themis, behold what I am suffering now, though I did bind that accursed one, my husband, by strong oaths to me? O, to see him and his bride some day brought to utter destruction, they and their house with them, for that they presume to wrong me thus unprovoked. O my father, my country, that I have left to my shame, after slaying my own brother.

NURSE. Do ye hear her words, how loudly she adjures Themis, oft invoked, and Zeus, whom men regard as keeper of their oaths? On no mere trifle surely will our mistress spend her rage.

CHORUS. Would that she would come forth for us to see, and listen to the words of counsel we might give, if haply she might lay aside the fierce fury of her wrath, and her temper stern. Never be my zeal at any rate denied my friends! But go thou and bring her hither outside the house, and tell her this our friendly thought; haste thee ere she do some mischief to those inside the house, for this sorrow of hers is mounting high.

NURSE. This will I do; but I have my doubts whether I shall persuade my mistress; still willingly will I undertake this trouble for you; albeit, she glares upon her servants with the look of a lioness with cubs, whenso anyone draws nigh to speak to her. Wert thou to call the men of old time rude uncultured boors thou wouldst not err, seeing that they devised their hymns for festive occasions, for banquets, and to grace the board, a pleasure to catch the ear, shed o'er our life, but no man hath found a way to allay hated grief by music and the minstrel's varied strain, whence arise slaughters and fell strokes of fate to o'erthrow the homes of men. And yet this were surely a gain, to heal men's wounds by music's spell, but why tune they their idle song where rich banquets are spread? for of itself doth the rich banquet, set before them, afford to men delight.

CHORUS. I heard a bitter cry of lamentation! loudly, bitterly she calls on the traitor of her marriage bed, her perfidious spouse; by grievous wrongs oppressed she invokes Themis, bride of Zeus, witness of oaths, who brought her unto Hellas, the land that fronts the strand of Asia, o'er the sea by night through ocean's boundless gate.

MEDEA. From the house I have come forth, Corinthian ladies, for fear lest you be blaming me; [4] for well I know that amongst men many by showing pride have gotten them an ill name and a reputation for indifference, both those who shun men's gaze and those who move amid the stranger crowd, and likewise they who choose a quiet walk in life. For there is no just discernment in the eyes of men, for they, or ever they have surely learnt their neighbour's heart, loathe him at first sight, though never wronged by him; and so a stranger most of all should adopt a city's views; nor do I commend that citizen, who, in the stubbornness of his heart, from churlishness resents the city's will.

But on me hath fallen this unforeseen disaster, and sapped my life; ruined I am, and long to resign the boon of existence, kind friends, and die. For he who was all the world to me, as well thou knowest, hath turned out the veriest villain, my own husband. Of all things that have life and sense we women are the most hapless creatures; first must we buy a husband at an exorbitant price, and o'er ourselves a tyrant set which is an evil worse than the first; and herein lies the most important issue, whether our choice be good or bad. For divorce is discreditable to women, nor can we disown our lords. Next must the wife, coming as she does to ways and customs new, since she hath not learnt the lesson in her home, have a diviner's eye to see how best to treat the partner of her life. If haply we perform these tasks with thoroughness and tact, and the husband live with us, without resenting the yoke, our life is a happy one; if not, 'twere best to die. But when a man is vexed with what he finds indoors, he goeth forth and rids his soul of its disgust, betaking him to some friend or comrade of like age; whilst we must needs regard his single self.

And yet they say we live secure at home, while they are at the wars, with their sorry reasoning, for I would gladly take my stand in battle array three times o'er, than once give birth. But enough! this language suits not thee as it does me; thou hast a city here, a father's house, some joy in life, and friends to share thy thoughts, but I am destitute, without a city, and therefore scorned by my husband, a captive I from a foreign shore, with no mother, brother, or kinsman in whom to find a new haven of refuge from this calamity. Wherefore this one boon and only this I wish to win from thee, thy silence, if haply I can some way or means devise to avenge me on my husband for this cruel treatment, and on the man who gave to him his daughter, and on her who is his wife. For though a woman be timorous enough in all else, and as regards courage, a coward at the mere sight of steel, yet in the moment she finds her honour wronged, no heart is filled with deadlier thoughts than hers.

CHORUS. This will I do; for thou wilt be taking a just vengeance on thy husband, Medea. That thou shouldst mourn thy lot surprises me not. But lo! I see Creon, king of this land coming hither, to announce some new resolve.

CREON. Hark thee, Medea, I bid thee take those sullen looks and angry thoughts against thy husband forth from this land in exile, and with thee take both thy children and that without delay, for I am judge in this sentence, and I will not return unto my house till I banish thee beyond the borders of the land.

MEDEA. Ah, me! now is utter destruction come upon me, unhappy that I am! For my enemies are bearing down on me full sail, nor have I any landing-place to come at in my trouble. Yet for all my wretched plight I will ask thee, Creon, wherefore dost thou drive me from the land?

CREON. I fear thee,—no longer need I veil my dread 'neath words,—lest thou devise against my child some cureless ill. Many things contribute to this fear of mine; thou art a witch by nature, expert in countless sorceries, and thou art chafing for the loss of thy husband's affection. I hear, too, so they tell me, that thou dost threaten the father of the bride, her husband, and herself with some mischief; wherefore I will take precautions ere our troubles come. For 'tis better for me to incur thy hatred now, lady, than to soften my heart and bitterly repent it hereafter.

MEDEA. Alas! this is not now the first time, but oft before, O Creon, hath my reputation injured me and caused sore mischief. Wherefore whoso is wise in his generation ought never to have his children taught to be too clever; for besides the reputation they get for idleness, they purchase bitter odium from the citizens. For if thou shouldst import new learning amongst dullards, thou will be thought a useless trifler, void of knowledge; while if thy fame in the city o'ertops that of the pretenders to cunning knowledge, thou wilt win their dislike. I too myself share in this ill-luck. Some think me clever and hate me, [others say I am too reserved, and some the very reverse];[5] others find me hard to please and not so very clever after all. Be that as it may, thou dost fear me lest I bring on thee something to mar thy harmony. Fear me not, Creon, my position scarce is such that I should seek to quarrel with princes. Why should I, for how hast thou injured me? Thou hast betrothed thy daughter where thy fancy prompted thee. No, 'tis my husband I hate, though I doubt not thou hast acted wisely herein. And now I grudge not thy prosperity; betroth thy child, good luck to thee, but let me abide in this land, for though I have been wronged I will be still and yield to my superiors.

CREON. Thy words are soft to hear, but much I dread lest thou art devising some mischief in thy heart, and less than ever do I trust thee now; for a cunning woman, and man likewise, is easier to guard against when quick-tempered than when taciturn. Nay, begone at once! speak me no speeches, for this is decreed, nor hast thou any art whereby thou shalt abide amongst us, since thou hatest me.

MEDEA. O, say not so! by thy knees and by thy daughter newly-wed, I do implore!

CREON. Thou wastest words; thou wilt never persuade me.

MEDEA. What, wilt thou banish me, and to my prayers no pity yield?

CREON. I will, for I love not thee above my own family.

MEDEA. O my country! what fond memories I have of thee in this hour!

CREON. Yea, for I myself love my city best of all things save my children.

MEDEA. Ah me! ah me! to mortal man how dread a scourge is love!

CREON. That, I deem, is according to the turn our fortunes take.

MEDEA. O Zeus! let not the author of these my troubles escape thee.

CREON. Begone, thou silly woman, and free me from my toil.

MEDEA. The toil is mine, no lack of it.

CREON. Soon wilt thou be thrust out forcibly by the hand of servants.

MEDEA. Not that, not that, I do entreat thee, Creon!

CREON. Thou wilt cause disturbance yet, it seems.

MEDEA. I will begone; I ask thee not this boon to grant.

CREON. Why then this violence? why dost thou not depart?

MEDEA. Suffer me to abide this single day and devise some plan for the manner of my exile, and means of living for my children, since their father cares not to provide his babes therewith. Then pity them; thou too hast children of thine own; thou needs must have a kindly heart. For my own lot I care naught, though I an exile am, but for those babes I weep, that they should learn what sorrow means.

CREON. Mine is a nature anything but harsh; full oft by showing pity have I suffered shipwreck; and now albeit I clearly see my error, yet shalt thou gain this request, lady; but I do forewarn thee, if to-morrow's rising sun shall find thee and thy children within the borders of this land, thou diest; my word is spoken and it will not lie. So now, if abide thou must, stay this one day only, for in it thou canst not do any of the fearful deeds I dread.

CHORUS. Ah! poor lady, woe is thee! Alas, for thy sorrows! Whither wilt thou turn? What protection, what home or country to save thee from thy troubles wilt thou find? O Medea, in what a hopeless sea of misery heaven hath plunged thee!

MEDEA. On all sides sorrow pens me in. Who shall gainsay this? But all is not yet lost! think not so. Still are there troubles in store for the new bride, and for her bridegroom no light toil. Dost think I would ever have fawned on yonder man, unless to gain some end or form some scheme? Nay, I would not so much as have spoken to him or touched him with my hand. But he has in folly so far stepped in that, though he might have checked my plot by banishing me from the land, he hath allowed me to abide this day, in which I will lay low in death three of my enemies—a father and his daughter and my husband too. Now, though I have many ways to compass their death, I am not sure, friends, which I am to try first. Shall I set fire to the bridal mansion, or plunge the whetted sword through their hearts, softly stealing into the chamber where their couch is spread? One thing stands in my way. If I am caught making my way into the chamber, intent on my design, I shall be put to death and cause my foes to mock. 'Twere best to take the shortest way—the way we women are most skilled in—by poison to destroy them. Well, well, suppose them dead; what city will receive me? What friendly host will give me a shelter in his land, a home secure, and save my soul alive? None. So I will wait yet a little while in case some tower of defence rise up for me; then will I proceed to this bloody deed in crafty silence; but if some unexpected mischance drive me forth, I will with mine own hand seize the sword, e'en though I die for it, and slay them, and go forth on my bold path of daring. By that dread queen whom I revere before all others and have chosen to share my task, by Hecate who dwells within my inmost chamber, not one of them shall wound my heart and rue it not. Bitter and sad will I make their marriage for them; bitter shall be the wooing of it, bitter my exile from the land. Up, then, Medea, spare not the secrets of thy art in plotting and devising; on to the danger. Now comes a struggle needing courage. Dost see what thou art suffering? 'Tis not for thee to be a laughing-stock to the race of Sisyphus [6] by reason of this wedding of Jason, sprung, as thou art, from a noble sire, and of the Sun-god's race. Thou hast cunning; and, more than this, we women, though by nature little apt for virtuous deeds, are most expert to fashion any mischief.

CHORUS. Back to their source the holy rivers turn their tide. Order and the universe are being reversed. 'Tis men whose counsels are treacherous, whose oath by heaven is no longer sure. Rumour shall bring a change o'er my life, bringing it into good repute. Honour's dawn is breaking for woman's sex; no more shall the foul tongue of slander fix upon us. The songs of the poets of old shall cease to make our faithlessness their theme. Phœbus, lord of minstrelsy, hath not implanted in our mind the gift of heavenly song, else had I sung an answering strain to the race of males, for time's long chapter affords many a theme on their sex as well as ours. With mind distraught didst thou thy father's house desert on thy voyage betwixt ocean's twin rocks, and on a foreign strand thou dwellest, thy bed left husbandless, poor lady and thou an exile from the land, dishonoured, persecuted. Gone is the grace that oaths once had. Through all the breadth of Hellas honour is found no more; to heaven hath it sped away. For thee no father's house is open, woe is thee! to be a haven from the troublous storm, while o'er thy home is set another queen, the bride that is preferred to thee.

JASON. It is not now I first remark, but oft ere this, how unruly a pest is a harsh temper. For instance, thou, hadst thou but patiently endured the will of thy superiors, mightest have remained here in this land and house, but now for thy idle words wilt thou be banished. Thy words are naught to me. Cease not to call Jason basest of men; but for those words thou hast spoken against our rulers, count it all gain that exile is thy only punishment. I ever tried to check the outbursts of the angry monarch, and would have had thee stay, but thou wouldst not forego thy silly rage, always reviling our rulers, and so thou wilt be banished. Yet even after all this I weary not of my goodwill, but am come with thus much forethought, lady, that thou mayst not be destitute nor want for aught, when, with thy sons, thou art cast out. Many an evil doth exile bring in its train with it; for even though thou hatest me, never will I harbour hard thoughts of thee.

MEDEA. Thou craven villain (for that is the only name my tongue can find for thee, a foul reproach on thy unmanliness)! comest thou to me, thou, most hated foe of gods, of me, and of all mankind? 'Tis no proof of courage or hardihood to confront thy friends after injuring them, but that worst of all human diseases loss of shame. Yet hast thou done well to come; for I shall ease my soul by reviling thee, and thou wilt be vexed at my recital. I will begin at the very beginning. I saved thy life, as every Hellene knows who sailed with thee aboard the good ship Argo, when thou wert sent to tame and yoke fire-breathing bulls, and to sow the deadly tilth. Yea, and I slew the dragon which guarded the golden fleece, keeping sleepless watch o'er it with many a wreathed coil, and I raised for thee a beacon of deliverance. Father and home of my free will I left and came with thee to Iolcos, 'neath Pelion's hills, for my love was stronger than my prudence. Next I caused the death of Pelias by a doom most grievous, even by his own children's hand, beguiling them of all their fear. All this have I done for thee, thou traitor! and thou hast cast me over, taking to thyself another wife, though children have been born to us. Hadst thou been childless still, I could have pardoned thy desire for this new union. Gone is now the trust I put in oaths. I cannot even understand whether thou thinkest that the gods of old no longer rule, or that fresh decrees are now in vogue amongst mankind, for thy conscience must tell thee thou hast not kept faith with me. Ah! poor right hand, which thou didst often grasp. These knees thou didst embrace! All in vain, I suffered a traitor to touch me! How short of my hopes I am fallen! But come, I will deal with thee as though thou wert my friend. Yet what kindness can I expect from one so base as thee? but yet I will do it, for my questioning will show thee yet more base. Whither can I turn me now? to my father's house, to my own country, which I for thee deserted to come hither? to the hapless daughters of Pelias? A glad welcome, I trow, would they give me in their home, whose father's death I compassed! My case stands even thus: I am become the bitter foe to those of mine own home, and those whom I need ne'er have wronged I have made mine enemies to pleasure thee. Wherefore to reward me for this thou hast made me doubly blest in the eyes of many a wife in Hellas; and in thee I own a peerless, trusty lord. O woe is me, if indeed I am to be cast forth an exile from the land, without one friend; one lone woman with her babes forlorn! Yea, a fine reproach to thee in thy bridal hour, that thy children and the wife who saved thy life are beggars and vagabonds! O Zeus! why hast thou granted unto man clear signs to know the sham in gold, while on man's brow no brand is stamped whereby to gauge the villain's heart?

CHORUS. There is a something terrible and past all cure, when quarrels arise 'twixt those who are near and dear.

JASON. Needs must I now, it seems, turn orator, and, like a good helmsman on a ship with close-reefed sails, weather that wearisome tongue of thine. Now, I believe, since thou wilt exaggerate thy favours, that to Cypris alone of gods or men I owe the safety of my voyage. Thou hast a subtle wit enough; yet were it a hateful thing for me to say that the Love-god constrained thee by his resistless shaft to save my life. However, I will not reckon this too nicely; 'twas kindly done, however thou didst serve me. Yet for my safety hast thou received more than ever thou gavest, as I will show. First, thou dwellest in Hellas, instead of thy barbarian land, and hast learnt what justice means and how to live by law, not by the dictates of brute force; and all the Hellenes recognize thy cleverness, and thou hast gained a name; whereas, if thou hadst dwelt upon the confines of the earth, no tongue had mentioned thee. Give me no gold within my halls, nor skill to sing a fairer strain than ever Orpheus sang, unless therewith my fame be spread abroad! So much I say to thee about my own toils, for 'twas thou didst challenge me to this retort. As for the taunts thou urgest against my marriage with the princess, I will prove to thee, first, that I am prudent herein, next chastened in my love, and last a powerful friend to thee and to thy sons; only hold thy peace. Since I have here withdrawn from Iolcos with many a hopeless trouble at my back, what happier device could I, an exile, frame than marriage with the daughter of the king? 'Tis not because I loathe thee for my wife—the thought that rankles in thy heart; 'tis not because I am smitten with desire for a new bride, nor yet that I am eager to vie with others in begetting many children, for those we have are quite enough, and I do not complain. Nay, 'tis that we—and this is most important—may dwell in comfort, instead of suffering want (for well I know that every whilom friend avoids the poor), and that I might rear my sons as doth befit my house; further, that I might be the father of brothers for the children thou hast born, and raise these to the same high rank, uniting the family in one, to my lasting bliss. Thou, indeed, hast no need of more children, but me it profits to help my present family by that which is to be. Have I miscarried here? Not even thou wouldest say so unless a rival's charms rankled in thy bosom. No, but you women have such strange ideas, that you think all is well so long as your married life runs smooth; but if some mischance occur to ruffle your love, all that was good and lovely erst you reckon as your foes. Yea, men should have begotten children from some other source, no female race existing; thus would no evil ever have fallen on mankind.

CHORUS. This speech, O Jason, hast thou with specious art arranged; but yet I think—albeit in saying so I betray indiscretion—that thou hast sinned in casting over thy wife.

MEDEA. No doubt I differ from the mass of men on many points; for, to my mind, whoso hath skill to fence with words in an unjust cause, incurs the heaviest penalty; for such an one, confident that he can cast a decent veil of words o'er his injustice, dares to practise it; and yet he is not so very clever after all. So do not thou put forth thy specious pleas and clever words to me now, for one word of mine will lay thee low. Hadst thou not had a villain's heart, thou shouldst have gained my consent, then made this match, instead of hiding it from those who loved thee.

JASON. Thou wouldest have lent me ready aid, no doubt, in this proposal, if I had told thee of my marriage, seeing that not even now canst thou restrain thy soul's hot fury.

MEDEA. This was not what restrained thee; but thine eye was turned towards old age, and a foreign wife began to appear discreditable to thee.

JASON. Be well assured of this: 'twas not for the woman's sake I wedded the king's daughter, my present wife; but, as I have already told thee, I wished to insure thy safety and to be the father of royal sons bound by blood to my own children—a bulwark to our house.

MEDEA. May that prosperity, whose end is woe, ne'er be mine, nor such wealth as would ever sting my heart!

JASON. Change that prayer as I will teach thee, and thou wilt show more wisdom. Never let happiness appear in sorrow's guise, nor, when thy fortune smiles, pretend she frowns!

MEDEA. Mock on; thou hast a place of refuge; I am alone, an exile soon to be.

JASON. Thy own free choice was this; blame no one else.

MEDEA. What did I do? Marry, then betray thee?

JASON. Against the king thou didst invoke an impious curse.

MEDEA. On thy house too maybe I bring the curse.

JASON. Know this, I will no further dispute this point with thee. But, if thou wilt of my fortune somewhat take for the children or thyself to help thy exile, say on; for I am ready to grant it with ungrudging hand, yea and to send tokens to my friends elsewhere who shall treat thee well. If thou refuse this offer, thou wilt do a foolish deed, but if thou cease from anger the greater will be thy gain.

MEDEA. I will have naught to do with friends of thine, naught will I receive of thee, offer it not to me; a villain's gifts can bring no blessing.

JASON. At least I call the gods to witness, that I am ready in all things to serve thee and thy children, but thou dost scorn my favours and thrustest thy friends stubbornly away wherefore thy lot will be more bitter still.

MEDEA. Away! By love for thy young bride entrapped, too long thou lingerest outside her chamber; go wed, for, if God will, thou shalt have such a marriage as thou wouldst fain refuse.

CHORUS. When in excess and past all limits Love doth come, he brings not glory or repute to man; but if the Cyprian queen in moderate might approach, no goddess is so full of charm as she. Never, O never, lady mine, discharge at me from thy golden bow a shaft invincible, in passion's venom dipped. On me may chastity, heaven's fairest gift, look[7] with a favouring eye; never may Cypris, goddess dread, fasten on me a temper to dispute, or restless jealousy, smiting my soul with mad desire for unlawful love, but may she hallow peaceful married life and shrewdly decide whom each of us shall wed. O my country, O my own dear home! God grant I may never be an outcast from my city, leading that cruel helpless life, whose every day is misery. Ere that may I this life complete and yield to death, ay, death; for there is no misery that doth surpass the loss of fatherland. I have seen with mine eyes, nor from the lips of others have I the lesson learnt; no city, not one friend doth pity thee in this thine awful woe. May he perish and find no favour, whoso hath not in him honour for his friends, freely unlocking his heart to them. Never shall he be friend of mine.

ÆGEUS. All hail, Medea! no man knoweth fairer prelude to the greeting of friends than this.

MEDEA. All hail to thee likewise, Ægeus, son of wise Pandion. Whence comest thou to this land?

ÆGEUS. From Phœbus' ancient oracle.

MEDEA. What took thee on thy travels to the prophetic centre of the earth?

ÆGEUS. The wish to ask how I might raise up seed unto myself.

MEDEA. Pray tell me, hast thou till now dragged on a childless life?

ÆGEUS. I have no child owing to the visitation of some god.

MEDEA. Hast thou a wife, or hast thou never known the married state?

ÆGEUS. I have a wife joined to me in wedlock's bond.

MEDEA. What said Phœbus to thee as to children?

ÆGEUS. Words too subtle for man to comprehend.

MEDEA. Surely I may learn the god's answer?

ÆGEUS. Most assuredly, for it is just thy subtle wit it needs.

MEDEA. What said the god? speak, if I may hear it.

ÆGEUS. He bade me "not loose the wineskin's pendent neck."[8]

MEDEA. Till when? what must thou do first, what country visit?

ÆGEUS. Till I to my native home return.

MEDEA. What object hast thou in sailing to this land?

ÆGEUS. O'er Trœzen's realm is Pittheus king.

MEDEA. Pelops' son, a man devout they say.

ÆGEUS. To him I fain would impart the oracle of the god.

MEDEA. The man is shrewd and versed in such-like lore.

ÆGEUS. Aye, and to me the dearest of all my warrior friends.

MEDEA. Good luck to thee! success to all thy wishes!

ÆGEUS. But why that downcast eye, that wasted cheek?

MEDEA. O Ægeus, my husband has proved a monster of iniquity.

ÆGEUS. What meanest thou? explain to me clearly the cause of thy despondency.

MEDEA. Jason is wronging me though I have given him no cause.

ÆGEUS. What hath he done? tell me more clearly.

MEDEA. He is taking another wife to succeed me as mistress of his house.

ÆGEUS. Can he have brought himself to such a dastard deed?

MEDEA. Be assured thereof; I, whom he loved of yore, am in dishonour now.

ÆGEUS. Hath he found a new love? or does he loathe thy bed?

MEDEA. Much in love is he! A traitor to his friend is he become.

ÆGEUS. Enough! if he is a villain as thou sayest.

MEDEA. The alliance he is so much enamoured of is with a princess.

ÆGEUS. Who gives his daughter to him? go on, I pray.

MEDEA. Creon, who is lord of this land of Corinth.

ÆGEUS. Lady, I can well pardon thy grief.

MEDEA. I am undone, and more than that, am banished from the land.

ÆGEUS. By whom? fresh woe this word of thine unfolds.

MEDEA. Creon drives me forth in exile from Corinth.

ÆGEUS. Doth Jason allow it? This too I blame him for.

MEDEA. Not in words, but he will not stand out against it. O, I implore thee by this beard and by thy knees, in suppliant posture, pity, O pity my sorrows; do not see me cast forth forlorn, but receive me in thy country, to a seat within thy halls. So may thy wish by heaven's grace be crowned with a full harvest of offspring, and may thy life close in happiness! Thou knowest not the rare good luck thou findest here, for I will make thy childlessness to cease and cause thee to beget fair issue; so potent are the spells I know.

ÆGEUS. Lady, on many grounds I am most fain to grant thee this thy boon, first for the gods' sake, next for the children whom thou dost promise I shall beget; for in respect of this I am completely lost.[9] 'Tis thus with me; if e'er thou reach my land, I will attempt to champion thee as I am bound to do. Only one warning I do give thee first, lady; I will not from this land bear thee away, yet if of thyself thou reach my halls, there shalt thou bide in safety and I will never yield thee up to any man. But from this land escape without my aid, for I have no wish to incur the blame of my allies as well.[10]

MEDEA. It shall be even so; but wouldst thou pledge thy word to this, I should in all be well content with thee.

ÆGEUS. Surely thou dost trust me? or is there aught that troubles thee?

MEDEA. Thee I trust; but Pelias' house and Creon are my foes.

Wherefore, if thou art bound by an oath, thou wilt not give[11] me up to them when they come to drag me from the land, but, having entered into a compact and sworn[12] by heaven as well, thou wilt become my friend and disregard their overtures. Weak is any aid of mine, whilst they have wealth and a princely house.

ÆGEUS. Lady, thy words show much foresight, so if this is thy will, I do not refuse. For I shall feel secure and safe if I have some pretext to offer to thy foes, and thy case too the firmer stands. Now name thy gods.

MEDEA. Swear by the plain of Earth, by Helios my father's sire, and, in one comprehensive oath, by all the race of gods.

ÆGEUS. What shall I swear to do, from what refrain? tell me that.

MEDEA. Swear that thou wilt never of thyself expel me from thy land, nor, whilst life is thine, permit any other, one of my foes maybe, to hale me thence if so he will.

ÆGEUS. By earth I swear, by the sun-god's holy beam and by all the host of heaven that I will stand fast to the terms I hear thee make.

MEDEA. 'Tis enough. If thou shouldst break this oath, what curse dost thou invoke upon thyself?

ÆGEUS. Whate'er betides the impious.

MEDEA. Go in peace; all is well, and I with what speed I may, will to thy city come, when I have wrought my purpose and obtained my wish.

CHORUS. May Maia's princely son go with thee on thy way to bring thee to thy home, and mayest thou attain that on which thy soul is set so firmly, for to my mind thou seemest a generous man, O Ægeus.

MEDEA. O Zeus, and Justice, child of Zeus, and sun-god's light, now will I triumph o'er my foes, kind friends; on victory's road have I set forth; good hope have I of wreaking vengeance on those I hate. For where we were in most distress this stranger hath appeared, to be a haven in my counsels; to him will we make fast the cables of our ship when we come to the town and citadel of Pallas. But now will I explain to thee my plans in full; do not expect to hear a pleasant tale. A servant of mine will I to Jason send and crave an interview; then when he comes I will address him with soft words, say, "this pleases me," and, "that is well," [even the marriage with the princess, which my treacherous lord is celebrating, and add "it suits us both, 'twas well thought out"];[13] then will I entreat that here my children may abide, not that I mean to leave them in a hostile land for foes to flout, but that I may slay the king's daughter by guile. For I will send them with gifts in their hands, carrying them unto the bride to save them from banishment, a robe of finest woof and a chaplet of gold. And if these ornaments she take and put them on, miserably shall she die, and likewise everyone who touches her; with such fell poisons will I smear my gifts. And here I quit this theme; but I shudder at the deed I must do next; for I will slay the children I have borne; there is none shall take them from my toils;

and when I have utterly confounded Jason's house I will leave the land, escaping punishment for my dear children's murder, after my most unholy deed. For I cannot endure the taunts of enemies, kind friends; enough! what gain is life to me? I have no country, home, or refuge left. O, I did wrong, that hour I left my father's home, persuaded by that Hellene's words, who now shall pay the penalty, so help me God. Never shall he see again alive the children I bore to him, nor from his new bride shall he beget issue, for she must die a hideous death, slain by my drugs. Let no one deem me a poor weak woman who sits with folded hands, but of another mould, dangerous to foes and well-disposed to friends; for they win the fairest fame who live their life like me.

CHORUS. Since thou hast imparted this design to me, I bid thee hold thy hand, both from a wish to serve thee and because I would uphold the laws men make.

MEDEA. It cannot but be so; thy words I pardon since thou art not in the same sorry plight that I am.

CHORUS. O lady, wilt thou steel thyself to slay thy children twain?

MEDEA. I will, for that will stab my husband to the heart.

CHORUS. It may, but thou wilt be the saddest wife alive.

MEDEA. No matter; wasted is every word that comes 'twixt now and then. (To the Nurse.) Ho! thou, go call me Jason hither, for thee I do employ on every mission of trust. No word divulge of all my purpose, as thou art to thy mistress loyal and likewise of my sex.

CHORUS. Sons of Erechtheus, heroes happy from of yore, children of the blessed gods, fed on wisdom's glorious food in a holy land ne'er pillaged by its foes, ye who move with sprightly step through a climate ever bright and clear, where, as legend tells, the Muses nine, Pieria's holy maids, were brought to birth by Harmonia with the golden hair; and poets sing how Cypris drawing water from the streams of fair-flowing Cephissus breathes[14] o'er the land a gentle breeze of balmy winds, and ever as she crowns her tresses with a garland of sweet rose-buds sends forth the Loves to sit by wisdom's side, to take a part in every excellence. How then shall the city of sacred streams, the land that welcomes those it loves, receive thee, the murderess of thy children, thee whose presence with others is a pollution? Think on the murder of thy children, consider the bloody deed thou takest on thee. Nay, by thy knees we, one and all, implore thee, slay not thy babes. Where[15] shall hand or heart find hardihood enough in wreaking such a fearsome deed upon thy sons? How wilt thou look upon thy babes, and still without a tear retain thy bloody purpose? Thou canst not, when they fall at thy feet for mercy, steel thy heart and dip in their blood thy hand.

JASON. I am come at thy bidding, for e'en though thy hate for me is bitter thou shalt not fail in this small boon, but I will hear what new request thou hast to make of me, lady.

MEDEA. Jason, I crave thy pardon for the words I spoke, and well thou mayest brook my burst of passion, for ere now we twain have shared much love. For I have reasoned with my soul and railed upon me thus, "Ah! poor heart! why am I thus distraught, why so angered 'gainst all good advice, why have I come to hate the rulers of the land, my husband too, who does the best for me he can, in wedding with a princess and rearing for my children noble brothers? Shall I not cease to fret? What possesses me, when heaven its best doth offer? Have I not my children to consider? do I forget that we are fugitives, in need of friends?" When I had thought all this I saw how foolish I had been, how senselessly enraged. So now I do commend thee and think thee most wise in forming this connexion for us; but I was mad, I who should have shared in these designs, helped on thy plans, and lent my aid to bring about the match, only too pleased to wait upon thy bride. But what we are, we are, we women, evil I will not say; wherefore thou shouldst not sink to our sorry level nor with our weapons meet our childishness.

I yield and do confess that I was wrong then, but now have I come to a better mind. Come hither, my children, come, leave the house, step forth, and with me greet and bid farewell to your father, be reconciled from all past bitterness unto your friends, as now your mother is for we have made a truce and anger is no more.

Enter the Children.

Take his right hand; ah me! my sad fate! when I reflect, as now, upon the hidden future. O my children, since there awaits you even thus a long, long life, stretch forth the hand to take a fond farewell. Ah me! how new[16] to tears am I, how full of fear! For now that I have at last released me from my quarrel with your father, I let the tear-drops stream adown my tender cheek.

CHORUS. From my eyes too bursts forth the copious tear; O, may no greater ill than the present e'er befall!

JASON. Lady, I praise this conduct, not that I blame what is past; for it is but natural to the female sex to vent their spleen against a husband when he trafficks in other marriages besides his own. [17] But thy heart is changed to wiser schemes and thou art determined on the better course, late though it be; this is acting like a woman of sober sense. And for you, my sons, hath your father provided with all good heed a sure refuge, by God's grace; for ye, I trow, shall with your brothers share hereafter the foremost rank in this Corinthian realm. Only grow up, for all the rest your sire and whoso of the gods is kind to us is bringing to pass. May I see you reach man's full estate, high o'er the heads of those I hate! But thou, lady, why with fresh tears dost thou thine eyelids wet, turning away thy wan cheek, with no welcome for these my happy tidings?

MEDEA. 'Tis naught; upon these children my thoughts were turned.

JASON. Then take heart; for I will see that it is well with them.

MEDEA. I will do so; nor will I doubt thy word; woman is a weak creature, ever given to tears.

JASON. Why prithee, unhappy one, dost moan o'er these children?

MEDEA. I gave them birth; and when thou didst pray long life for them, pity entered into my soul to think that these things must be. But the reason of thy coming hither to speak with me is partly told, the rest will I now mention. Since it is the pleasure of the rulers of the land to banish me, and well I know 'twere best for me to stand not in the way of thee or of the rulers by dwelling here, enemy as I am thought unto their house, forth from this land in exile am I going, but these children,—that they may know thy fostering hand, beg Creon to remit their banishment.

JASON. I doubt whether I can persuade him, yet must I attempt it.

MEDEA. At least do thou bid thy wife ask her sire this boon, to remit the exile of the children from this land.

JASON. Yea, that will I; and her methinks I shall persuade, since she is a woman like the rest.

MEDEA. I too will aid thee in this task, for by the children's hand I will send to her gifts that far surpass in beauty, I well know, aught that now is seen 'mongst men, a robe of finest tissue and a chaplet of chased gold. But one of my attendants must haste and bring the ornaments hither. Happy shall she be not once alone but ten thousandfold, for in thee she wins the noblest soul to share her love, and gets these gifts as well which on a day my father's sire, the Sun-god, bestowed on his descendants. My children, take in your hands these wedding gifts, and bear them as an offering to the royal maid, the happy bride; for verily the gifts she shall receive are not to be scorned.

JASON. But why so rashly rob thyself of these gifts? Dost think a royal palace wants for robes or gold? Keep them, nor give them to another. For well I know that if my lady hold me in esteem, she will set my price above all wealth.

MEDEA. Say not so; 'tis said that gifts tempt even gods; and o'er men's minds gold holds more potent sway than countless words. Fortune smiles upon thy bride, and heaven now doth swell her triumph; youth is hers and princely power; yet to save my children from exile I would barter life, not dross alone. Children, when ye are come to the rich palace, pray your father's new bride, my mistress, with suppliant voice to save you from exile, offering her these ornaments the while; for it is most needful that she receive the gifts in her own hand. Now go and linger not; may ye succeed and to your mother bring back the glad tidings she fain would hear!

CHORUS. Gone, gone is every hope I had that the children yet might live; forth to their doom they now proceed. The hapless bride will take, ay, take the golden crown that is to be her ruin; with her own hand will she lift and place upon her golden locks the garniture of death. Its grace and sheen divine will tempt her to put on the robe and crown of gold, and in that act will she deck herself to be a bride amid the dead. Such is the snare whereinto she will fall, such is the deadly doom that waits the hapless maid, nor shall she from the curse escape. And thou, poor wretch, who to thy sorrow art wedding a king's daughter, little thinkest of the doom thou art bringing on thy children's life, or of the cruel death that waits thy bride. Woe is thee! how art thou fallen from thy high estate!

Next do I bewail thy sorrows, O mother hapless in thy children, thou who wilt slay thy babes because thou hast a rival, the babes thy husband hath deserted impiously to join him to another bride.

ATTENDANT. Thy children, lady, are from exile freed, and gladly did the royal bride accept thy gifts in her own hands, and so thy children made their peace with her.

MEDEA. Ah!

ATTENDANT. Why art so disquieted in thy prosperous hour? Why turnest thou thy cheek away, and hast no welcome for my glad news?

MEDEA. Ah me!

ATTENDANT. These groans but ill accord with the news I bring.

MEDEA. Ah me! once more I say.

ATTENDANT. Have I unwittingly announced some evil tidings? Have I erred in thinking my news was good?

MEDEA. Thy news is as it is; I blame thee not.

ATTENDANT. Then why this downcast eye, these floods of tears?

MEDEA. Old friend, needs must I weep; for the gods and I with fell intent devised these schemes.

ATTENDANT. Be of good cheer; thou too of a surety shalt by thy sons yet be brought home again.

MEDEA. Ere that shall I bring others to their home, ah! woe is me!

ATTENDANT. Thou art not the only mother from thy children reft. Bear patiently thy troubles as a mortal must.

MEDEA. I will obey; go thou within the house and make the day's provision for the children. O my babes, my babes, ye have still a city and a home, where far from me and my sad lot you will live your lives, reft of your mother for ever; while I must to another land in banishment, or ever I have had my joy of you, or lived to see you happy, or ever I have graced your marriage couch, your bride, your bridal bower, or lifted high the wedding torch. Ah me! a victim of my own self-will. So it was all in vain I reared you, O my sons; in vain did suffer, racked with anguish, enduring the cruel pangs of childbirth. 'Fore Heaven I once had hope, poor me! high hope of ye that you would nurse me in my age and deck my corpse with loving hands, a boon we mortals covet; but now is my sweet fancy dead and gone; for I must lose you both and in bitterness and sorrow drag through life. And ye shall never with fond eyes see your mother more, for o'er your life there comes a change. Ah me! ah me! why do ye look at me so, my children? why smile that last sweet smile? Ah me! what am I to do? My heart gives way when I behold my children's laughing eyes. O, I cannot; farewell to all my former schemes; I will take the children from the land, the babes I bore. Why should I wound their sire by wounding them, and get me a twofold measure of sorrow? No, no, I will not do it. Farewell my scheming! And yet what am I coming to? Can I consent to let those foes of mine escape from punishment, and incur their mockery? I must face this deed. Out upon my craven heart! to think that I should even have let the soft[18] words escape my soul. Into the house, children! and whoso feels he must not be present at my sacrifice, must see to it himself; I will not spoil my handiwork. Ah! ah! do not, my heart, O do not do this deed! Let the children go, unhappy one, spare the babes! For if they live, they will cheer thee in our exile there[19] Nay, by the fiends of hell's abyss, never, never will I hand my children over to their foes to mock and flout. Die they must in any case, and since 'tis so, why I, the mother who bore them, will give the fatal blow. In any case their doom is fixed and there is no escape. Already the crown is on her head, the robe is round her, and she is dying, the royal bride; that do I know full well. But now since I have a piteous path to tread, and yet more piteous still the path I send my children on, fain would I say farewell to them. O my babes, my babes, let your mother kiss your hands. Ah! hands I love so well, O lips most dear to me! O noble form and features of my children, I wish ye joy, but in that other land, for here your father robs you of your home. O the sweet embrace, the soft young cheek, the fragrant breath! my children! Go, leave me; I cannot bear to longer look upon ye; my sorrow wins the day. At last I understand the awful deed I am to do; but passion, that cause of direst woes to mortal man, hath triumphed o'er my sober thoughts.

CHORUS. Oft ere now have I pursued subtler themes and have faced graver issues than woman's sex should seek to probe; but then e'en we aspire to culture, which dwells with us to teach us wisdom; I say not all; for small is the class amongst women—(one maybe shalt thou find 'mid many)—that is not incapable of culture. And amongst mortals I do assert that they who are wholly without experience and have never had children far surpass in happiness those who are parents. The childless, because they have never proved whether children grow up to be a blessing or curse to men are removed from all share in many troubles; whilst those who have a sweet race of children growing up in their houses do wear away, as I perceive, their whole life through; first with the thought how they may train them up in virtue, next how they shall leave their sons the means to live; and after all this 'tis far from clear whether on good or bad children they bestow their toil. But one last crowning woe for every mortal man I now will name; suppose that they have found sufficient means to live, and seen their children grow to man's estate and walk in virtue's path, still if fortune so befall,[20] comes Death and bears the children's bodies off to Hades. Can it be any profit to the gods to heap upon us mortal men beside our other woes this further grief for children lost, a grief surpassing all?

MEDEA. Kind friends, long have I waited expectantly to know how things would at the palace chance. And lo! I see one of Jason's servants coming hither, whose hurried gasps for breath proclaim him the bearer of some fresh tidings.

Mes. Fly, fly, Medea! who hast wrought an awful deed, transgressing every law; nor leave behind or sea-borne bark or car that scours the plain.

MEDEA. Why, what hath chanced that calls for such a flight of mine?

MESSENGER. The princess is dead, a moment gone, and Creon too, her sire, slain by those drugs of thine.

MEDEA. Tidings most fair are thine! Henceforth shalt thou be ranked amongst my friends and benefactors.

MESSENGER.Ha! What? Art sane? Art not distraught, lady, who nearest with joy the outrage to our royal house done, and art not at the horrid tale afraid?

MEDEA. Somewhat have I, too, to say in answer to thy words. Be not so hasty, friend, but tell the manner of their death, for thou wouldst give me double joy, if so they perished miserably.

MESSENGER. When the children twain whom thou didst bear came with their father and entered the palace of the bride, right glad were we thralls who had shared thy griefs, for instantly from ear to ear a rumour spread that thou and thy lord had made up your former quarrel. One kissed thy children's hands, another their golden hair, while I for very joy went with them in person to the women's chambers. Our mistress, whom now we do revere in thy room, cast a longing glance at Jason, ere she saw thy children twain; but then she veiled her eyes and turned her blanching cheek away, disgusted at their coming; but thy husband tried to check his young bride's angry humour with these words: "O, be not angered 'gainst thy friends; cease from wrath and turn once more thy face this way, counting as friends whomso thy husband counts, and accept these gifts, and for my sake crave thy sire to remit these children's exile." Soon as she saw the ornaments, no longer she held out, but yielded to her lord in all; and ere the father and his sons were far from the palace gone, she took the broidered robe and put it on, and set the golden crown about her tresses, arranging her hair at her bright mirror, with many a happy smile at her breathless counterfeit. Then rising from her seat she passed across the chamber, tripping lightly on her fair white foot, exulting in the gift, with many a glance at her uplifted ankle.[21] When lo! a scene of awful horror did ensue. In a moment she turned pale, reeled backwards, trembling in every limb, and sinks upon a seat scarce soon enough to save herself from falling to the ground. An aged dame, one of her company, thinking belike it was a fit from Pan[22] or some god sent, raised a cry of prayer, till from her mouth she saw the foam-flakes issue, her eyeballs rolling in their sockets, and all the blood her face desert; then did she raise a loud scream far different from her former cry. Forthwith one handmaid rushed to her father's house, another to her new bridegroom to tell his bride's sad fate, and the whole house echoed with their running to and fro. By this time would a quick walker have made the turn in a course of six plethra[23] and reached the goal, when she with one awful shriek awoke, poor sufferer, from her speechless trance and oped her closed eyes, for against her a twofold anguish was warring. The chaplet of gold about her head was sending forth a wondrous stream of ravening flame, while the fine raiment, thy children's gift, was preying on the hapless maiden's fair white flesh; and she starts from her seat in a blaze and seeks to fly, shaking her hair and head this way and that, to cast the crown therefrom; but the gold held firm to its fastenings, and the flame, as she shook her locks, blazed forth the more with double fury. Then to the earth she sinks, by the cruel blow o'ercome, past all recognition now save to a father's eye; for her eyes had lost their tranquil gaze, her face no more its natural look preserved, and from the crown of her head blood and fire in mingled stream ran down; and from her bones the flesh kept peeling off beneath the gnawing of those secret drugs, e'en as when the pine-tree weeps its tears of pitch, a fearsome sight to see. And all were afraid to touch the corpse, for we were warned by what had chanced. Anon came her hapless father unto the house, all unwitting of her doom, and stumbles o'er the dead, and loud he cried, and folding his arms about her kissed her, with words like these the while, "O my poor, poor child, which of the gods hath destroyed thee thus foully? Who is robbing me of thee, old as I am and ripe for death? O my child, alas! would I could die with thee!" He ceased his sad lament, and would have raised his aged frame, but found himself held fast by the fine-spun robe as ivy that clings to the branches of the bay, and then ensued a fearful struggle. He strove to rise, but she still held him back; and if ever he pulled with all his might, from off his bones his aged flesh he tore. At last he gave it up, and breathed forth his soul in awful suffering; for he could no longer master the pain. So there they lie, daughter and aged sire, dead side by side, a grievous sight that calls for tears. And as for thee, I leave thee out of my consideration, for thyself must discover a means to escape punishment. Not now for the first time I think this human life a shadow; yea, and without shrinking I will say that they amongst men who pretend to wisdom and expend deep thought on words do incur a serious charge of folly; for amongst mortals no man is happy; wealth may pour in and make one luckier than another, but none can happy be.

CHORUS. This day the deity, it seems, will mass on Jason, as he well deserves, a heavy load of evils. Woe is thee, daughter of Creon! We pity thy sad fate, gone as thou art to Hades' halls as the price of thy marriage with Jason.

MEDEA. My friends, I am resolved upon the deed; at once will I slay my children and then leave this land, without delaying long enough to hand them over to some more savage hand to butcher. Needs must they die in any case; and since they must, I will slay them—I, the mother that bare them. O heart of mine, steel thyself! Why do I hesitate to do the awful deed that must be done? Come, take the sword, thou wretched hand of mine! Take it, and advance to the post whence starts thy life of sorrow! Away with cowardice! Give not one thought to thy babes, how dear they are or how thou art their mother. This one brief day forget thy children dear, and after that lament; for though thou wilt slay them yet they were thy darlings still, and[24] I am a lady of sorrows.

CHORUS. O earth, O sun whose beam illumines all, look, look upon this lost woman, ere she stretch forth her murderous hand upon her sons for blood; for lo! these are scions of thy own golden seed, and the blood of gods is in danger of being shed by man. O light, from Zeus proceeding, stay her, hold her hand, forth from the house chase this fell bloody fiend by demons led. Vainly wasted were the throes thy children cost thee; vainly hast thou born, it seems, sweet babes, O thou who hast left behind thee that passage through the blue Symplegades, that strangers justly hate. Ah! hapless one, why doth fierce anger thy soul assail? Why[25] in its place is fell murder growing up? For grievous unto mortal men are pollutions that come of kindred blood poured on the earth, woes to suit each crime hurled from heaven on the murderer's house.

1st Son (within). Ah, me; what can I do? Whither fly to escape my mother's blows?

2nd Son (within). I know not, sweet brother mine; we are undone.

CHORUS. Didst hear, didst hear the children's cry? O lady, born to sorrow, victim of an evil fate! Shall I enter the house? For the children's sake I am resolved to ward off the murder.

1ST SON (within). Yea, by heaven I adjure you; help, your aid is needed.

2ND SON (within). Even now the toils of the sword are closing round us.

CHORUS. O hapless mother, surely thou hast a heart of stone or steel to slay the offspring of thy womb by such a murderous doom. Of all the wives of yore I know but one who laid her hand upon her children dear, even Ino,[26] whom the gods did madden in the day that the wife of Zeus drove her wandering from her home. But she, poor sufferer, flung herself into the sea because of the foul murder of her children, leaping o'er the wave-beat cliff, and in her death was she united to her children twain. Can there be any deed of horror left to follow this? Woe for the wooing of women fraught with disaster! What sorrows hast thou caused for men ere now!

JASON. Ladies, stationed near this house, pray tell me is the author of these hideous deeds, Medea, still within, or hath she fled from hence? For she must hide beneath the earth or soar on wings towards heaven's vault, if she would avoid the vengeance of the royal house. Is she so sure she will escape herself unpunished from this house, when she hath slain the rulers of the land? But enough of this! I am forgetting her children. As for her, those whom she hath wronged will do the like by her; but I am come to save the children's life, lest the victim's kin visit their wrath on me, in vengeance for the murder foul, wrought by my children's mother.

CHORUS. Unhappy man, thou knowest not the full extent of thy misery, else had thou never said those words.

JASON. How now? Can she want to kill me too?

CHORUS. Thy sons are dead; slain by their own mother's hand.

JASON. O God! what sayest thou? Woman, thou hast sealed my doom.

CHORUS. Thy children are no more; be sure of this[.]

JASON. Where slew she them; within the palace or outside?

CHORUS. Throw wide the doors and see thy children's murdered corpses.

JASON. Haste, ye slaves, loose the bolts, undo the fastenings, that I may see the sight of twofold woe, my murdered sons and her, whose blood in vengeance I will shed.

[Medea in mid air, on a chariot drawn by dragons; the children's corpses by her.

MEDEA. Why shake those doors and attempt to loose their bolts, in quest of the dead and me their murderess? From such toil desist. If thou wouldst aught with me, say on, if so thou wilt; but never shalt thou lay hand on me, so swift the steeds the sun, my father's sire, to me doth give to save me from the hand of my foes.

JASON. Accursed woman! by gods, by me and all mankind abhorred as never woman was, who hadst the heart to stab thy babes, thou their mother, leaving me undone and childless; this hast thou done and still dost gaze upon the sun and earth after this deed most impious. Curses on thee! I now perceive what then I missed in the day I brought thee, fraught with doom, from thy home in a barbarian land to dwell in Hellas, traitress to thy sire and to the land that nurtured thee. On me the gods have hurled the curse that dogged thy steps, for thou didst slay thy brother at his hearth ere thou cam'st aboard our fair ship "Argo." Such was the outset of thy life of crime; then didst thou wed with me, and having born me sons to glut thy passion's lust, thou now hast slain them. Not one amongst the wives of Hellas e'er had dared this deed; yet before them all I chose thee for my wife, wedding a foe to be my doom, no woman, but a lioness fiercer than Tyrrhene Scylla in nature. But with reproaches heaped a thousandfold I cannot wound thee, so brazen is thy nature. Perish, vile sorceress, murderess of thy babes! Whilst I must mourn my luckless fate, for I shall ne'er enjoy my new-found bride, nor shall I have the children, whom I bred and reared, alive to say the last farewell to me; nay, I have lost them.

MEDEA. To this thy speech I could have made a long retort, but Father Zeus knows well all I have done for thee, and the treatment thou hast given me. Yet thou wert not ordained to scorn my love and lead a life of joy in mockery of me, nor was thy royal bride nor Creon, who gave thee a second wife, to thrust me from this land and rue it not. Wherefore, if thou wilt, call me e'en a lioness, and Scylla, whose home is in the Tyrrhene land; for I in turn have wrung thy heart, as well I might.

JASON. Thou, too, art grieved thyself, and sharest in my sorrow.

MEDEA. Be well assured I am; but it relieves my pain to know thou canst not mock at me.

JASON. O my children, how vile a mother ye have found!

MEDEA. My sons, your father's feeble lust has been your ruin!

JASON. 'Twas not my hand, at any rate, that slew them.

MEDEA. No, but thy foul treatment of me, and thy new marriage.

JASON. Didst think that marriage cause enough to murder them?

MEDEA. Dost think a woman counts this a trifling injury?

JASON. So she be self-restrained; but in thy eyes all is evil.

MEDEA. Thy sons are dead and gone. That will stab thy heart.

JASON. They live, methinks,[27] to bring a curse upon thy head.

MEDEA. The gods know, whoso of them began this troublous coil.

JASON. Indeed, they know that hateful heart of thine.

MEDEA. Thou art as hateful. I am aweary of thy bitter tongue.

JASON. And I likewise of thine. But parting is easy.

MEDEA. Say how; what am I to do? for I am fain as thou to go.

JASON. Give up to me those dead, to bury and lament.

MEDEA. No, never! I will bury them myself, bearing them to Hera's sacred field, who watches o'er the Cape, that none of their foes may insult them by pulling down their tombs; and in this land of Sisyphus I will ordain hereafter a solemn feast and mystic rites to atone for this impious murder. Myself will now to the land of Erechtheus, to dwell with Ægeus, Pandion's son. But thou, as well thou mayest, shalt die a caitiff's death, thy head[28]crushed 'neath a shattered relic of Argo, when thou hast seen the bitter ending of my marriage.

JASON. The curse of our sons' avenging spirit and of Justice, that calls for blood, be on thee!

MEDEA. What god or power divine hears thee, breaker of oaths and every law of hospitality?

JASON. Fie upon thee! cursed witch! child-murderess!

MEDEA. To thy house! go, bury thy wife.

JASON. I go, bereft of both my sons.

MEDEA. Thy grief is yet to come; wait till old age is with thee too.

JASON. O my dear, dear children!

MEDEA. Dear to their mother, not to thee.

JASON. And yet thou didst slay them?

MEDEA. Yea, to vex thy heart.

JASON. One last fond kiss, ah me! I fain would on their lips imprint.

MEDEA. Embraces now, and fond farewells for them but then a cold repulse!

JASON. By heaven I do adjure thee, let me touch their tender skin.

MEDEA. No, no! in vain this word has sped its flight.

JASON. O Zeus, dost hear how I am driven hence; dost mark the treatment I receive from this she-lion, fell murderess of her young? Yet so far as I may and can, I raise for them a dirge, and do adjure[29] the gods to witness how thou hast slain my sons, and wilt not suffer me to embrace or bury their dead bodies. Would I had never begotten them to see thee slay them after all!

CHORUS. Many a fate doth Zeus dispense, high on his Olympian throne; oft do the gods bring things to pass beyond man's expectation; that, which we thought would be, is not fulfilled, while for the unlooked-for god finds out a way; and such hath been the issue of this matter.

FOOTNOTES

1. πεσσοὺς literally the game itself; here explained by the Scholiast as the place where it was habitually played.

2. So MSS. ἀπλήστου. Elmsley, whom many editors have followed, proposed ἀπλάτου="terrible."

3. καὶ πότνι᾽Ἄρτεμι, corrupt and pointless. The reading here adopted by the translator is καὶ πόσις, ἄρτι με, suggested by Munro (Journal of Philology, No. 22, p. 275) πόσις=Zeus.

4. To extract any satisfactory meaning from this passage, as it stands in our editions, seems an almost impossible task, to judge from the attempts at present made. I have not ventured to alter Paley's text, or proposed interpretation, unsatisfactory as it seems to me. Verrall's emendations, though bold in the extreme, do at least make the Greek intelligible, and to his ingenious note I would refer the curious.

5. This line is inclosed by most editors in brackets as an interpolation from 808 below, where it is in place.

6. Sisyphus was the founder of the royal house of Corinth.

7. Verrall proposes to read στέγοι "protect," for MSS. στέργοι.

8. i.e., enjoined strict chastity.

9. The Schol. gives two interpretations of φροῦδος. (1) "I am ruined as far as begetting children goes." (2) "I am entirely devoted to doing so." Neither is satisfactory owing to want of parallel passages.

10. i.e., as well as Jason.

11. To avoid the very doubtful form μεθεῖς = μεθείης some read μεθεῖ᾽ ἄν.

12. Reading ἐνώμοτος. Hermann changes καὶ into μὴ. A simpler change, supported by a Schol., and one MS., would be to read ἀνώμοτος="whereas if thou only make a verbal compact, without oath, thou mightest be persuaded," etc. The whole passage is, as it stands, probably corrupt; numerous emendations have been proposed. If the above emendation be adopted, it will be necessary to alter οὐκ ἄν πίθοιο for which Munro proposed ὀκνῶν πίθοιο="and fearing their demands of surrender thou mightest yield." Wecklein, τάχ' ἄν πίθοι σε (adopted by Nauck), is tempting.

13. Porson condemns these two lines.

14. Reading χώρας with Reiske. The passage is corrupt, and possibly some word is lost.

15. Of the numerous emendations of this corrupt passage, Nauck's τέκνον for τέκνοις is the simplest, if it goes far enough. Verrall suggests that a word has fallen out after the second ἤ and conjectures μένος ἁ τέχναν. This is not less satisfactory than most of the emendations.

16. ἀρτίδακρυς. The Schol. explains this word as "ready to shed tears," but ἄρτι, as Mr. Evelyn Abbott points out, can scarcely bear such a meaning. (Cf., in Heberden's edition of the Medea, his note.)

17. i.e. ἀλλοίους. This word is not elsewhere used in tragedy, and has therefore been suspected. Heimsoethius conjectures παρεμπολῶντι δευτέρους, Dindorf δώμασιν.

18. Reading πρόεσθαι for which Badham proposes πρόσεσθαι, "indulge my mind in gentle thoughts."

19. At Athens.

20. Reading κυοήσει (Ald. et Schol.). The MSS. vary between κυρήσας, σαι σει.

21. τένοντ' ἐς ὀρθὸν σκοπουμένη, (1) she stretches out her foot to see how the robe falls over it (Paley), (2) she stands on tiptoe and looks back to see how the dress hangs behind = erecto pede (Pflugk).

22. Any sudden seizure was ascribed to Pan's agency.

23. The reading is doubtful, still more the meaning. The conjecture ἀνελθών is adopted here, with Musgrave's ἄν ἥπτετο for ἀνθήπτετο. ἀνελθὼν κῶλον ἑκπλέθρου δρόμου. This would mean, her swoon lasted as long as a man would take to go and return the distance of six plethra. The κῶλον then must be the 'limb, lap' of the course up to the turning post.

24. The construction is intentionally irregular. Her emotion prevents a grammatical completion of the sentence.

25. This use of ἀμείβεται is so unusual that the passage is open to grave suspicion. The three following lines are extremely confused and probably corrupt. Weil proposes ἐπέγειρεν for 'επὶ γαῖαν; var. lect. for ξυνῳδὰ is ξύνοιδα

26. This is Euripides' version of the legend, not the usual one; which makes Athamas the father go mad and kill one son, while Ino leaps into the sea with the other.

27. Reading οἶμαι with Tyrrwhitt.

28. Legend told how Jason was slain by a beam falling on him as he lay asleep under the shadow of his ship Argo.

29. κἀπιθεάζω, Blomfield's emendation for MSS. κἀπιθοάζω

CPSIA information can be obtained at www.ICGtesting.com
Printed in the USA
BVOW05s1622210615

405464BV00013BA/370/P